T0130461

The Dough-NUT$

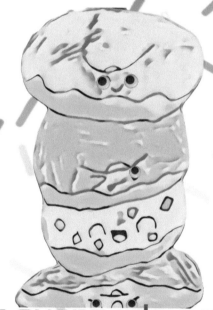

Illustrations and inspirations by Emma Gardner
Presented by Richard Gardner
Created by GOD

© 2023 Richard Gardner. All rights reserved.

No part of this book may be reproduced, stored in a retrieval system, or transmitted by any means without the written permission of the author.

AuthorHouse™
1663 Liberty Drive
Bloomington, IN 47403
www.authorhouse.com
Phone: 833-262-8899

Because of the dynamic nature of the Internet, any web addresses or links contained in this book may have changed since publication and may no longer be valid. The views expressed in this work are solely those of the author and do not necessarily reflect the views of the publisher, and the publisher hereby disclaims any responsibility for them.

Any people depicted in stock imagery provided by Getty Images are models, and such images are being used for illustrative purposes only.
Certain stock imagery © Getty Images.

This book is printed on acid-free paper.

ISBN: 979-8-8230-0353-7 (sc)
ISBN: 979-8-8230-0357-5 (e)

Print information available on the last page.

Published by AuthorHouse 03/24/2023

authorHOUSE®

Contents

1
"The Dough-NUT$ Shop"

1

The Doughnut Shop

My favorite place. The sweet doughnut shop.
I can't even wait. I skip and I hop.
I'm in such a hurry. I don't want to stop.
Not a care or a worry. Not the first trip for me.
To the place where sugar pours like rain on the street.
A blizzard of frosting on every treat.

I look in the window.
Oh that sweet bread aroma!
My eyes get real wide, like that track at Daytona.
Hearts racing now!
Beating fast. I'm an engine.
I run through the door.
I've got school, did I mention?
My mom sent me out on my way to the store.
Get us some milk, a few eggs, pretty sure.

But, here I am, at the old donut shop.
I'm feeling some guilt, but I'm not gonna stop.
Because I've got 50 cents from my old Grandpop-pop.
For doing some laundry and running a mop.

So I don't feel guilty about what I'm gonna do.
They'll be gone 'fore I get home.
There'll be no real proof.
My plan is so sweet. I've got nothing to lose.
All of the treats...now which one to choose?

2

Choices

So many choices. They all look so sweet.
The sugary sprinkles. The frosting so neat.

The shapes and the sizes.
Some long and some short.
Little ones I can munch on.
Ones that make faces contort.
When I eat the whole treat in one giant bite.
Oh the looks that I get. They say I'm not right.

I hope I can swallow.
Mom says, "Swallow your pride."
"Don't need to be choosy. Be grateful."
I'll try.
But I want every one. Guess I'm greedy.
I lied.

Maybe, I could have a new one each day?
Munchkins on Monday.
On Tuesdays I'll say,
"Hey, what's the deal with all that creme filling?"
Donuts everyday!
I'll just say it.
You're silly!

Brings me to Wednesday.
Long John's are the cure.
Chocolate or Vanilla?
Love 'em both that's for sure.

Hmmmm
And on Thursday...
I could try something new.
A throwback to what my dear Grandma likes too.
A Persian with nuts on the top.
It's "health" food.

On Friday I'll smile, though my belly got swole.
Take a break here on Saturday?
It's the weekend.
Let's roll!

On to the cinnamon swirls in my mind.
Not gonna pretend that everything's fine.
Oh my goodness! How can they smell even better?
On Saturday mornings no matter the weather.

I get to the donut shop with a grin.
Throw down my dollar. I feel it again.
Now what is it going to be on this day?
I'll eat this eclair.
Ah Bon jur. As they say.

Sunday brings me all the way back around.
I'm learning too much,
of what I love
gets me down.

Here at the shop. It's Monday again.
Not gonna stop, but **this** time...
for my friends.

So many choices
I know what to do...
Get a dozen or so,
Then give them to you.

3

One Day Old

The choices are plenty.
A problem.
I sigh.
The donuts are many.
Too many to try.
If I had the dough though...
I'd enjoy every kind.

You pick one, then I...
Will grab a few too.
Thirteen is the number...
That Bakers all use.

Got to the cashier, where I needed to pay.
What's in my pocket?
A few bills and some change.

That's when I see them...
Out of view from the rest.
They look just like new.
What's the difference?
I guessed.

Maybe they are...
The treats set aside.
For some special person who'll *be* coming by.
Put in a place, so no one will buy.
Or
Perhaps they're a gift to a poor starving fool.
A present that's wrapped.
Now they'll be happy too.

But alas, what I found
Is the wonderful truth.
They're called "Day Old" donuts.
They're just one day old.
How great it must be...
to not know they are sold.

Unfortunate though that they go so unnoticed.
Little money for those.
Even though that's the motive.

And what's the big deal?
Are they poisonous now?
"Throw'em away! They're no good to us."
Wow!

The *only* thing that we want is the best.
One day it goes by, and we move on to the next.
Forgetting about what needs to be done.
Who will make sure that everyone can get some?

And come to find out that these gems are devalued.
Half the price now.
So, I made a new plan soon.

When I think about it, it seems that I find.
Being born yesterday...
Means opening your mind.

What to do?
It's your choice?
Which way?
Wants or needs?

It's my turn.
Use my voice.

Then the Baker asks me.

I think for a second...

"One **"Day-Old"** please."

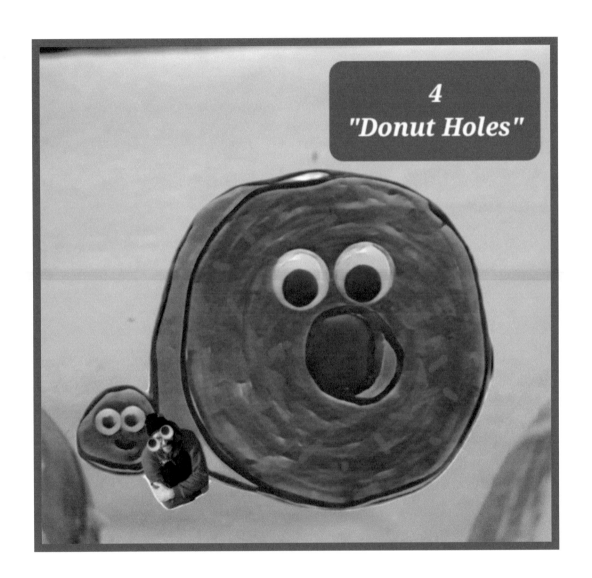

4

Donut Holes

There are many kinds of donuts I find.
A world full of flavors. What should I try?
They say that variety spices up life.
Might as well try each kind that you like.

There are lots of types, differences though...
It's common to see...
Donuts with a hole.

Why is it there?
What is the reason?
Too big for my hand to wear like a ring
And...
Too small for my wrist.
Now I'm getting crazy.
Seems like extra work.
I know Baker's aren't lazy.

Working hard every morning.
Making the dough.
Creating masterpieces...
from circles with holes.

Each one is just right. So unique are the types.
We're all very different, and somehow alike.
A hole in the middle. No way we can hide so.
We're full of so little. So fill it we try though.

So what's going on?
I've made a conclusion.
Sometimes there's no answer, or simple solution.
Made sense in the past, so now we keep doing.
Things that could end up being our ruin.

Is there a point to what we all do?
These Munchkins are great.
I enjoy them all too.

5
"On Display"

Pink Iced Donut with Sprinkles
290 cal each 99¢

15

5

On Display

What a wonderful view. I like what I see.
Take a look at what's new. It's smelling so sweet.

I walked in and I saw donuts of all kinds.
The shapes and the colors. Sprinkles on my mind.
Rows upon rows of pastries sublime.

Saturday morning. What a great day!
A window full of decisions to make.
Taking it easy. Is *the* only way.
They all look so good.
But there's more oh they say.

It's what's on the inside that matters for me.
Creme filing's good, hiding what's sweet.
Who cares how it works?
Cuz yeast will still leaven.
And all are just different versions of heaven.

Well, so much for my diet.
I'm telling on me.
Now is the end of me eating healthy.

Taste buds are working.
Saliva starts flowing.
How will I choose?
I've got to get going.

I know what I want.
To feel good today.
Now it's my turn.
Now who's on display?
If I'm truly honest I like it that way.

Give me a second.
I know what I need.
I look in your eyes.
A smile can be sweet.

And Donuts are great!
A masterpiece to behold.
When they're on display.
Worth way more than gold.

And what would you pay for what you can't display?
I read a book this one time, well the cover was great.

6
"Long-John"

6

"Long" John

Vanilla- "Hey John, What's up? You seem like you're blue. Looking long. Your chocolate icing *is* dripping too."

Chocolate- "Well John, I guess. Well, I guess I don't know. It's *dark* in my world. Your icing's like snow. It's different for me."

V- "Well that is for sure.
Do you want to talk? About what you've been feeling."
"We've got time to walk, before this big meeting"

C- "Do you know what it's like to be…compared to dirt?
Some make jokes about me."

V- "Well I've been called worse."

C- "Maybe you know what it's like to be me. To have them all laugh, then stop when I see.

I know that deep down, my inside's not jelly. No secrets to hide. Put me in your belly!!

But of course it has spread,
I was in bad taste.
That I was like eating a tube poop paste."

V- "I'll stop you right there. You've got it all wrong.
Sure, bad jokes were told, but you truly belong."

C- "What are you trying to say here big fella?"

V- "I'll show you we're similar. Chocolate and vanilla."

19

C- "What do you mean? *I'm* just like *you?*"

V- 'We *both* taste real sweet."

C- "Yeah…Well…That's true."

V- "And what do you mean, your world is so dark? You're right next to me. We're barely apart. And oh by the way. I think you're a star.
Or whatever you'd call a coco dessert.
I'd be proud to have your stain on my shirt."

C- "I hear what you're saying. Now I know that I'm good. Thank you for helping me feel like I should."

V- "Glad I could help. Now, get ready. It's go-time.
This meeting has coffee. That means that it's showtime!"

7
"Coffee&Donuts"

Coffee&Donuts

Donuts go with coffee.
Honey mixes with tea.
Good conversations with you.
You taking slow walks with me.

Our words are great when they're kind.
Poems go great when they rhyme.
And who knows what great things we'll make?
Imagination.
Sublime.

Superheros go great with their powers.
Look up. They're flying so high.
Sunshine goes great with showers.
Oh yeah, rainbows will shine.
Just Like when we get together
Good Vibes me make every time.

See...
One dish of Blue Moon ice cream,
Really, needs only 2 spoons.
My wishes are just like a dream.
Hope I'll be seeing you soon.

Heart emojis go great when I send em.
Road trips go great with friends too.
Turn it up. The beat never ends and...
My heart seems to be beating for you.

And my favorite song would go great...
f it never ended. That's true.

And making no plans tonight.
Goes with *me* chillin with *you*.
And yeah, a man is alright.
He needs a woman who knows what to do.

Just look what we make when together.
Seems that It's great every time.
Coffee and Donuts forever!
Like when you and I are combined.

8

Donut Envy

I don't care what's for breakfast.
I don't care what for dinner.

I don't care what's for dessert.
Donuts are the winner!

I don't care where they made it.
I don't care if you hate it.

I don't care what's inside.
Or where you display it.

I don't mind...when they call me names.
I don't hate it.

I don't care about rules.
When it comes to my treats.

I don't care what they're called.
They are all calling me!

I don't care if it's a cruller or scone.
Cinnamon rolls are better when warm.
And I don't care if it's cake or it's raised.
Because...
I don't really care...how it was made

I don't care what you pick.
I'll have more than a lick.

I don't care what it is called.
I don't care if they roll them *into* little balls.

I don't care if it has icing or plain.
Or
Who ate the last one?
I know who you'll blame.

I don't really care what they say about me.
They don't know I'm aware...
Of their...*Donut Envy.*

9
"Take a Number"

9

Take a number

It's Saturday.
This place is packed!
So I take a number at this great Donut shop.

Sigh and I wait
They're glazed and they're stacked.
I just gotta wonder, who *is* at the top?

The top of this list. How'd *they* get to be...
The lucky ones. The ones who will eat.
All of the treats.
Oooh. My jealousy...
Is gonna get the best of me.

I watch them all take.
Take all of my wants.
Until all I am left with...
All of my thoughts!
And what is left of my patience...
It stalls.

It's at its ending.
Who'll stop this theft?
My mind it is bending.
If there's *any* left.

The time it stands still.
Will my number get called today?
I gotta go!
My Mom said, "Don't disobey."

Can I convince you?
That I am a prince who...
Requires one...of *everything!*
I'll have 200.
I said that I'm hungry!
And one day they say...That *I* may be King.

I ran out of my tricks.
I can accept this.
So many things that I can't control.

Then the Baker brings.
A fresh trays of rings.
Glazed and golden, freshly baked dough.

I guess that it pays.
I'm learning to wait.
For all that I what, and then I'll get more.
Of what it is...
That I'm waiting for?

10
"Rolling in the Dough"

30

10

Rolling in the Dough

I got some dough now.
Rolling 'round this town.
Need a quick pick me up.
Cuz I'm feeling down.

And what do I see?
What's *that* before me?

They're kneading in the dough. To make a pastry.
A raspberry treat. Or maybe, cream cheese.
Put frosting on top. Mmm. It's complete!

What goes in the dough?
Flour, sugar, eggs, oh!
Love is the secret...
To make donuts. You know?

But, what about dough?
For needs and wants though?
"Well. How much do I need in this life just to grow?"

Not sure if it's so.
Till I sift through on my own.
Then it's so clear.
All my dough is on loan.

And I'm nuts not to see.
That dough is so free.
Someone told me once…
That it comes from a seed.

It's getting real tricky…
For him and for her.
When it gets real sticky…
Add some flour. And stir.
And take a deep breath.
It's all just a blur.

When we take what is needed.
Ask neighbors for ingredients.
Mix it all up.
We enjoy life's experiences.

11
"The Persian"

The Persian

I see the donut. The one that I like.
And it is not like…any other type.

It's unique just like me.
And, choices can be…
So over-whelming.
Just look around…
Believe me. You'll see.

How each kind's not like the other.
There's no need to compare.
Like you and me, you're my Brother.
My Mom taught me not to stare.

Just because, *it's* not the same.
I take a breath. What's *this* donut's name?

Oh they've been called so many things.
The Berry Frosted to The Boston Cream.
Names they can change for everyone.
You can blame me when it is all done.

But the Persian *is* the one.
Frosted and nuts on top.
Cinnamon sticky bun.
Used to eat with my Grandpop.

And where are they *really* from?
Some magic place?
Lands so far off.
From outer space.

A treat so great…Fit for a king.
Or a General in the army.
And, yes here's the thing.
Most of these stories seem alarming.

But,
Deep inside it's *all* the same.
Dough is what's got me insane.
And what's it *all* worth to you?
Love is free, but so's the truth.

Where's it from? Or what's inside?
Yeah you can run, but you can't hide.
Or tell a lie. Just digging holes.
Give it a try, and then you'll know.

The Persian *is* such a mystery.
A Donut with such a history.
Too long ago to really know.
Might as well enjoy the dough.

12
"Too Much"

12

Too Much

Too much.
Too much of what?

Some say one donut is just enough.
And any more goes to your gut.
Or to my butt.
And oh yeah, right to my thighs.
Man oh man. When will I try?

To gain some power,
From *Will* I guess?
Because they say he does his best.
To balance things, like wants and needs.
Who is this dude? And, can we meet?
Because he must know how to be free.
From wanting more of *everything*.
I'll just have one, turns right into three.

Too much donuts makes me a fool.
But add some nuts, makes a new rule.
Healthy treats?
Come on. You too?
Out of touch with reality.
They call it lust.
For dough. Just greed.

Simple though is the way.
To make some dough, and celebrate!
We just create our own cool version.
Don't hesitate. Each day I'm learning.
Bout what it takes to make a dream.
There ain't no doubt.
Know what I mean?

Well if you don't...Don't worry none.
Here, have a donut, and I'll have one.

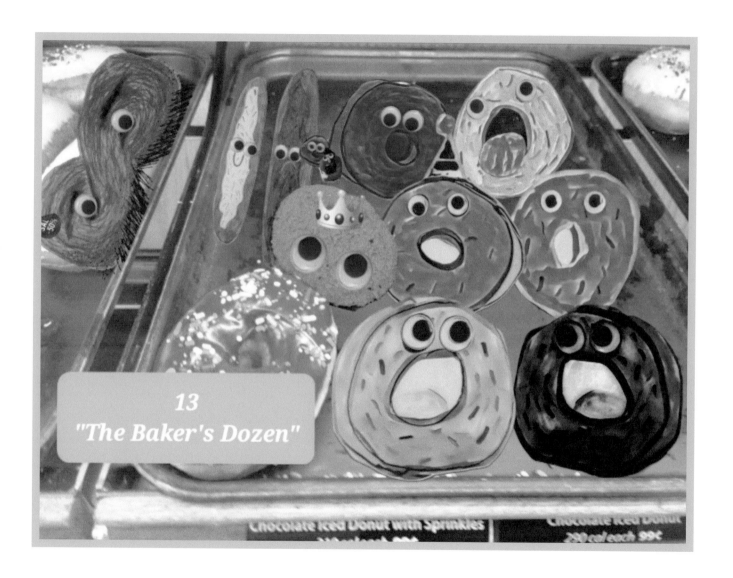

13
"The Baker's Dozen"

13

The Baker's Dozen

"The Baker's Dozen"
A group oh so strange.
People don't know what to say.
Or what to do. To have a clue.
About this sweet band of who is whose.

These rebel treats.
Oddly unique.
They're like no other.
Let's not compete.
"The Baker's Dozen" 13 they say.
They *ARE* for eating, not just display.
So here they are, no more delay:

What's "The Wonut?"
Don't you all know?
A fried, then frosted waffle.
Oh?!

Aaaay…Oh!
Who's the new kid on the block here though?
Oh, ay, here we've got…
Got the right stuff. A real good spot…

"The Boston Cream."
Chocolate up top.
Custard between.
Get outta here!
Know what I mean?

"The Maple Bacon" just like a dream.
Because bacon makes everything.
Better than it was before.
You disagree? I'll have some more.
Sprinkle it everywhere.
With Maple frosting? Oh, yes they dare.
The Baker doesn't have any cares.
He makes creations for us to share.

Like "The Bear Claw," big and wide.
Perfect size and glazed just right.
A ridge on top like fingers or toes.
If I have two, thing is, I'm full!

Speaking of *me* getting fuller.
Next up. Let's see...it's "The French Cruller."

Not like other Krullers that is.
Like a cream puff and churro made kids.
Fancy enough...to come here from France.
Call my bluff. Who knows.
I can't...
Even tell anymore.
Where they are from, so I'll adore.
Everyone. And, does it matter?
"This French Cruller" just gets me fatter.

And mon ami, "Cronuts" they *are* from France.
Croissant that's glazed. Why would you pass? .
It's flaky and fun, like someone I know.
Stay till you're done.
Au revoir. There you go.

"The Apple Fritter," takes me way back.
Grandma's pie. Makes me say that...
Simple things give us joy.
A little sugar for girls and boys.
The little pieces of apples in dough.

I'm dreaming I guess.
Don't wake me up though.

"The Persian."
The General.
The cream of the crop.
Cinnamon. Better when there's nuts on top.
Who would dare challenge?
Who is insane?
Enough. Will you manage, to just stay the same?
You compare?
Heaven's sake!
What a pair that they make.
When the dough and the nuts mix it up in this way.

Say what,
"Spudnuts"...are outta this world. Well, I think.
But what's the deal with the nuts and the things?
There are no nuts here. Or so I will say.
The spud makes its way, all the way to the stage.
Inside of that German Baker's dough.
And what was to hide? I've learned...potatoes!

Oh what a treat. It's called "The Spudnut."
Oh, it's so sweet. No need for ketchup!

They say there's a donut...
Called "The Devil's Food."
And do you know what?
Hey, that sounds real good.
Or is it bad? I'll eat just one.
Then, I am done.
Okay. Okay.
Just 2 or 3.
Maybe 12 or...okay, maybe 13.

No! I'll show dad. How it is done.
How temptation...it can be won.

Oh, but then…
My wants *are* on display.
No. It's no sin. "**The Devil's Food**," has its way.

"**The Twisted Donut**" *has* fluffy dough.
Fried to golden perfection and rolled…
In cinnamon and sugar. Now. Whoa!!

In the Philippines, they're called Shakoy.
It seems that this treat brings them much joy.
The perfect twist gives me some shivers.
I learned that some gifts should just get delivered.
And I will accept them. *Every* time.
A twist of our fate. See what we'll find.

"**The Cream Cheese Danish**" is next on the list.
A treat that's so heinous, just turn and dismiss.
Or run away. From *all* of your fears.
Just let it all go. So that we can clear…
The elephant, that sits in the room.
Say, "Yes you can." It's never too soon.
To enjoy these fine pastries.
I guess they're from Denmark.
Hey, I am not lazy. It's just hard to start.

But here we all go. And we'll never know.
Why we were told….
To hold onto everything, just like it's gold.

No more control…the sprinkles can flow.
What's wrong? Yeah. You're right.
But, these donuts, they make me…
They make me feel nice.

The sugar rushes like…Rocket fuel.
I BLAST OFF!
And there is one more…right in the box.
What a surprise! A real nice delight!

"The Baker's Dozen"...13.
YES! Alright!!

A little weird, yeah, like me.
And, I KNOW I'M JUST RIGHT.
I hope you can see.
It's been my delight.

Printed in the United States
by Baker & Taylor Publisher Services